BLACK BEAR, BROWN CUB

Sandra Grace Walker

Butterfly Language Publishing

Copyright © 2022 Sandra Grace Walker

All rights reserved. No part of this book may be reproduced in any form or by any electronic or mechanical means, including information storage and retrieval systems, without permission in writing from the publisher, except by reviewers, who may quote brief passages in a review.

ISBN 978-1-7371309-3-2 (Paperback Edition)
ISBN 978-1-7371309-4-9 (Hardcover Edition)

Library of Congress Control Number
2022905010

The veiwpoints, opinions and beliefs expressed herein are solely of the author. Such views, opinions and perspectives are intended to convey a life story are based on the recollections about their lives and are not intended to malign any individual, religion, ethnic group or company.

Printed and bound in the United States of America
First printing May 2022

Published by Butterfly Language Publishing
Hampstead, MD 21074

Visit www.butterflylanguagepublishing.com

Butterfly Language Publishing

Dedication

I dedicate this book to all the boys and girls around the world. Home is where your heart is. Family are those that love you!

Acknowledgment

Vaughn this book was inspired by you. I pray you receive it as a blessing from above.

You were born north of here in a deep blizzard of snow.

Just at that moment,
something happened on that
miraculous day.

A glimmer of light, a flash of hope illuminated the sky as she was mesmerized

Something way up high flew by, like a burst of lighting in the cloudless sky, and then she noticed a stork land by her side.

The Mama brown bear replied "I have to make a hard decision, and I am scared of what to do. My decision will affect all that is involved, especially my baby cub too."

"I need to find a family that will love him through and through.

A family that will love him as their own, and he knows he would never be alone."

The stork flew high and low, far and wide;

miles for miles across the nation's skies.

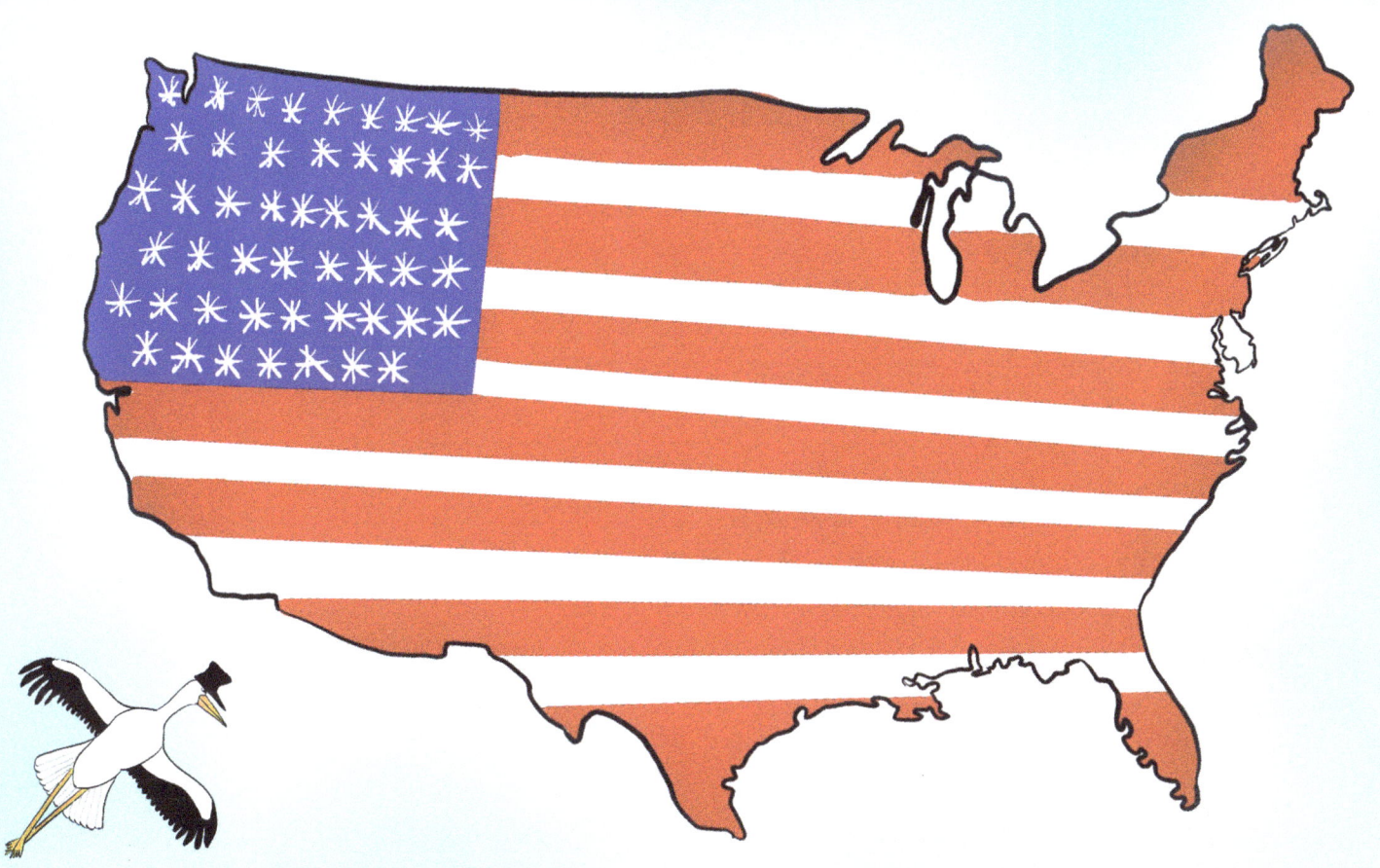

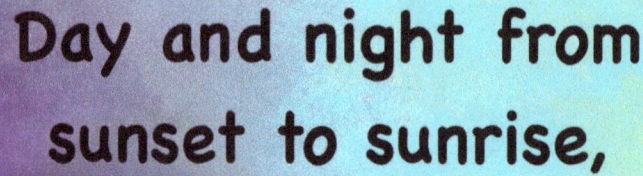

Day and night from sunset to sunrise,

Looking for that perfect family for the brown bear cub to love.

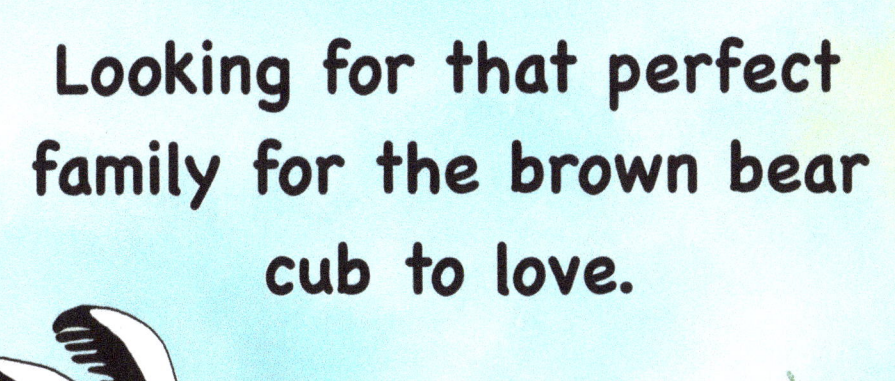

When a stork landed at my den and asked me, How I was?

Elated by the idea and grateful for the kind gesture,

I immediately said yes, I would love to.

That I was chosen to do the rest, to love you, to protect you, to nurture you for the rest of your life. You are my brown bear cub that I love.

We are a family built from above and based on unconditional love.

Always remember

You are SPECIAL!
You are GREAT!
You are DESERVING!
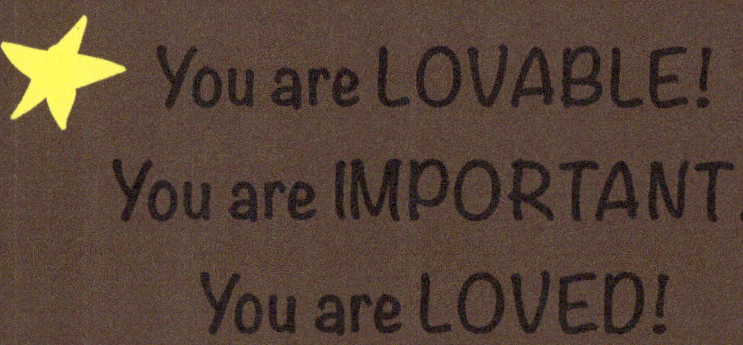
You are LOVABLE!
You are IMPORTANT!
You are LOVED!
You are a GIFT!
You are a BLESSING!
You are ENOUGH!

DRAW A PICTURE OF YOUR FAMILY

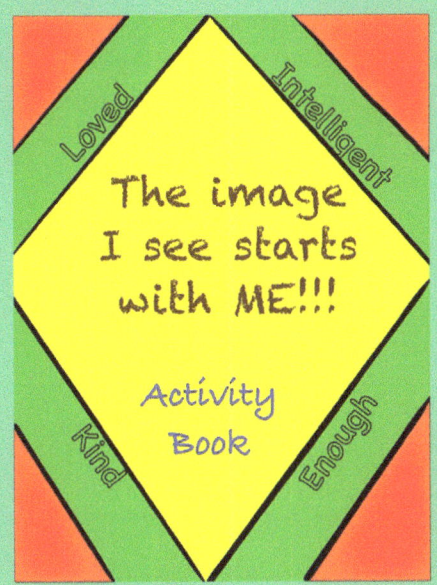

Hand drawn activity book with over 50 positive affirmations for our children to see and feel.

This children's picture book promotes self-love and hope for our brown children by letting them know that being different is beautiful.

Stay connected with us:

butterflylanguagepublishing.com
butterflylanguagepublishing@gmail.com
https://facebook.com/sandragrace.walker
https://www.instagram.com/sandra_grace_walker

www.ingramcontent.com/pod-product-compliance
Lightning Source LLC
Chambersburg PA
CBHW050805220426
43209CB00088BA/1635